I Can Grow Plants!

Rosemary Jennings

INFOMAX COMMON CORE READERS

Rosen Classroom™

New York

Published in 2013 by The Rosen Publishing Group, Inc.
29 East 21st Street, New York, NY 10010

Book Design: Michael Harmon

Photo Credits: Cover Yuri Arcurs/Shutterstock.com; p. 4 Evlakhov Valeriy/Shutterstock.com; p. 5 Ivonne Wierink/Shutterstock.com; p. 6 JGI/Jamie Grill/Blend Images/Getty Images; p. 7 Meryll/Shutterstock.com; p. 8 Szasz-Fabian Ilka Erika/Shutterstock.com; p. 9 Dreamframer/Shutterstock.com; p. 10 Smit/Shutterstock.com; p. 11 Katrina Leigh/Shutterstock.com; p. 12 DenisNata/Shutterstock.com; p. 13 Elanamiv/Shutterstock.com; p. 14 italianestro/Shutterstock.com; p. 15 1000 Words Images/Shutterstock.com; p. 16 Stephen Aaron Rees/Shutterstock.com; p. 17 Urbanowicz/Shutterstock.com; p. 18 Kovalchuk Oleksandr/Shutterstock.com; p. 19 manfredxy/Shutterstock.com; p. 20 Yaruta Igor/Shutterstock.com; p. 21 norr/Shutterstock.com.

ISBN: 978-1-4488-8989-1
6-pack ISBN: 978-1-4488-8990-7

Manufactured in the United States of America

CPSIA Compliance Information: Batch #WS12RC: For further information contact Rosen Publishing, New York, New York at 1-800-237-9932.

Word Count: 198

Contents

Plants are living things
that grow in the ground.

Plants can be big or small.

Plants can grow inside or outside.

Growing plants is easy,
but they need a lot of love.

When I grow plants,
I start with seeds.

The seeds go into the ground.

I cover them with dirt.

I can't see my seeds when I'm done.

Plants need a lot of water.

They need water to grow.

In a few days, the plants
will grow above the ground.

My plants get bigger every day.

First, they grow stems.

Then, the plants grow leaves.

The leaves use the sun to make food.

I water my plants every day.

They get hot in the sun.

Some of my plants grow flowers.

Flowers make my house look pretty.

Now my plants are fully grown.

It took a lot of work.

Do you want to know something cool?

Sometimes I find bugs on my plants!

The bugs use my plants as a home.
That's where they eat.

The bugs help make new plants.

This is an important job.

The new plants will be
just like my first plants.

I like growing plants.

What kinds of plants do you know?

How a Plant Grows

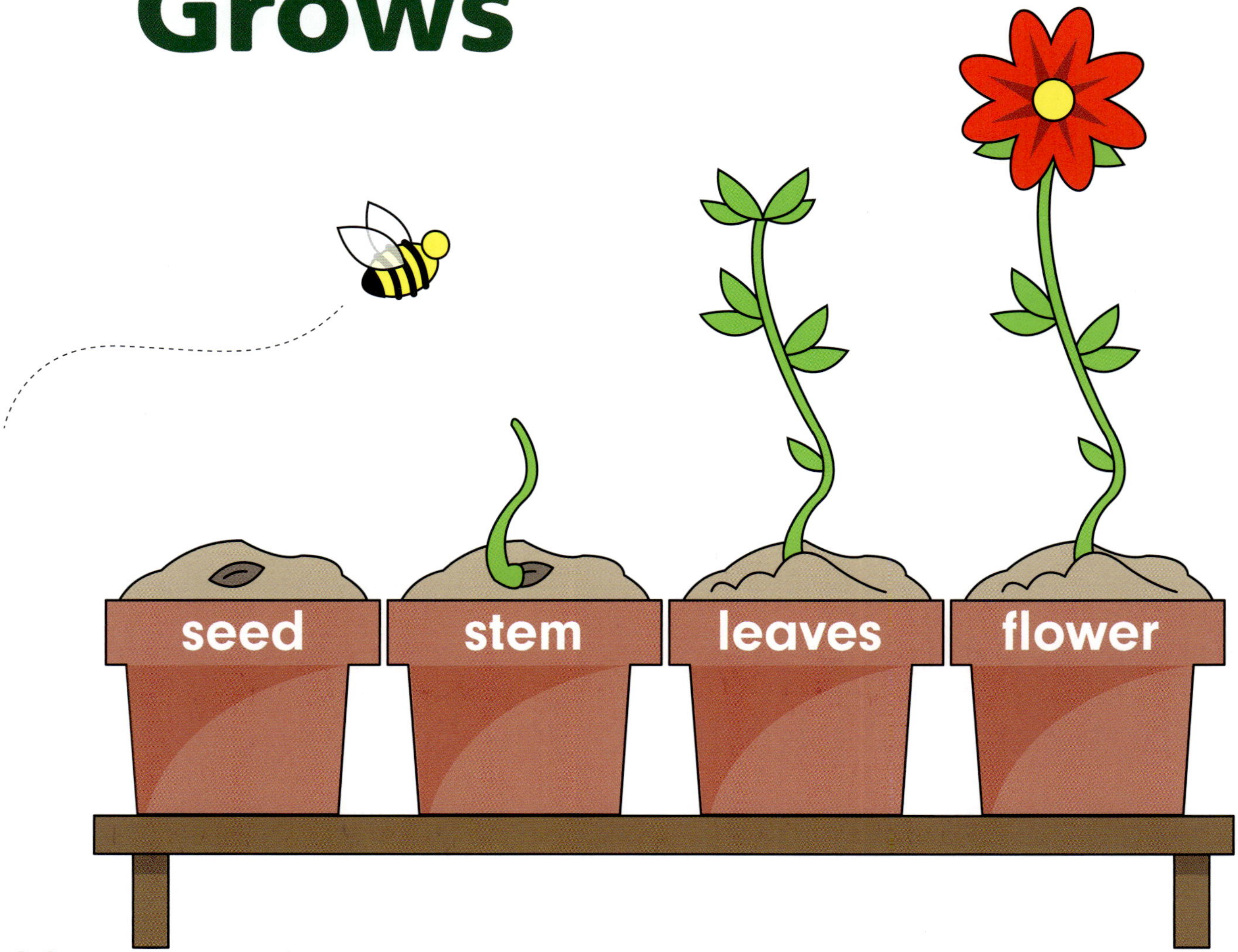

Words to Know

flowers

leaves

seeds

stem

Index